HOW TO POO
YOUR WAY TO THE TOP

MATS & ENZO

PRION

CONTENTS

INTRODUCTION

Life in a company is a mixture of rules, teamwork, hierarchy, anarchy, sympathy, resentment and responsibility. Within this tangle of rites and rituals employees try to achieve their personal goals.

Corporate life has become so complex that there are now specialist magazines that give advice on how to survive it, not to mention hundreds of books written on the topic. It is clearly essential to read all of this advice if you want to succeed. We must educate ourselves on how to behave and how to be useful within a company.

Many star employees, executives, directors and so on invest much of their personal time in such reading. In their quest for perfection, these overachievers read everything that comes into their hands. Yet many of them will have overlooked the most important facet of corporate life. The sad truth remains that none of the books currently available give any advice whatsoever on the one place that many consider taboo: the workplace toilets.

What is the problem? None of the researchers, journalists, authors or philosophers have devoted their time to the question of the comfort break. Yet going to the toilet is a real dilemma in the life of the modern employee. It is here that, confronted with the most primitive need, the hierarchy of the company is levelled; it's a place where colleagues, bosses, secretaries and others gain equal footing.

But smells, noise, frequency of use, and toilets that don't work are all factors that can ruin a career.

It is highly likely that the first serious study to be made on this subject will reveal the thousands of misadventures that happen in this seemingly innocent place have led to cancelled promotions, total loss of credibility for executives with their secretaries and humiliating dramas that can never be forgotten yet must never be discussed. How many executives from big companies with separate bathrooms for ladies and for gentlemen have lost their credibility when they moved to head up a smaller company and were faced with a unisex bathroom? How many others will find their ascent to the top terminated due to lack of education on this subject? And how many secretaries have given their bosses porcine nicknames just because they met in the toilet at a bad moment?

It takes only one second, one misadventure in the toilets of your workplace to ruin forever the image that you have built up in the eyes of your colleagues and your superiors! I am also certain that all of you have used some carefully devised strategies when going to the bathroom at work (going on a different floor or using the toilets at the other end of the hall for example). This is because you know, deep inside, that you have nothing to gain by going to the toilet, but everything to lose!

Fortunately, you now have this book in your hands: the global reference on the subject. It has already saved tens of thousands of careers on all continents and is about to save hundreds of thousands more. Thanks to the advice that it gives, your corporate destiny will never be shattered by a trip to your workplace toilets.

It provides all the strategies needed to operate as adroitly as possible when going to the toilet, while you are in it and when you are leaving it. Finally, it unveils the tricks of the pros on the matter. Many techniques were inspired by the tactics of the SAS, CIA agents and ninja assassins, but also included are contributions from anonymous inventive people who applied some pearls of creativity to prevent career suicide. After reading this book, you will know how to confront any terrain, avoid traps in any kind of infrastructure, even the oldest ones, and will understand the techniques necessary to confront even the trickiest bathroom situation with complete confidence.

Our goal is to guarantee you safe visits to the toilet, without any danger to your career.

In the last chapter of this book, we will unveil how you can poo your way to the top. You will discover previously unknown tips and the fastest way to success.

Enjoy reading… wherever you may be*!

MATS

"A man who is at the top is a man who has the habit of getting to the bottom."

Joseph E. Rogers

* Some people actually read in their living rooms, and not just in bed like you do.

THE EXPERT: TOM HAYATT

Tom Hayatt has become the indisputable authority on the subject of toilets in the workplace. It was he who first shed light on the issue in the prestigious *Management Journal of the Massachusetts Institute of Technology* in the 1987 article, "Real Social Working Dynamics for Water Closets". At first he was not taken too seriously due to the perceived triviality of the subject, but in 1992 he was finally recognized by his peers, in no small part because of the prestigious award given to him that year: The Golden Toilet Brush.

His name was also circulated as a possible candidate for a Nobel Prize in economics. He is often associated with the acronym TML3S, a mnemonic tool used by many executives to remind them of the dangers that lurk on the way to the toilets and to avoid any faux pas. TML3S stands for 'Trace, Movement, Light, Shadow, Sound, Smell'.

Today, Tom Hayatt has circled the globe to speak at conferences. For the past ten years his exclusive lectures on 'Pooing at Work' have been an immense success in the United States, despite the $2,000 entry fee per participant. In these lectures he unveils his method, which is appreciated by all who have difficulties pooing at work. He is also regularly consulted on the proper positioning of toilets in high-rise buildings. We are honoured to work with such an expert. His wise and exclusive advice will impress you.

In the second part of the book, he will explain to you how an employee can turn to new responsibilities if he is good at pooing at work. At the beginning of his career, before he became an indisputable authority on the subject of toilets in the workplace, the rise of Tom Hayatt was more than impressive. He managed to go from being a simple trainee to become the CEO of a multinational company by pooing his way to the top. Read this book and you will be able to follow the same fast track! We are immensely honoured that Tom Hayatt has agreed once again to provide his expertise and vision for this book. His advice has changed our lives and it is about to change yours.

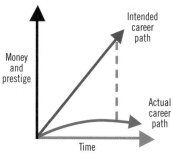

Not pooing at work the right way

> "How can a man take on new responsibilities if he struggles to poo at work? It matters not how small or large a job you currently have, if you haven't trained to poo the right way, you've made your promotion difficult if not impossible."
>
> Tom Hayatt

CHAPTER 1

Basic skills

Just as you wouldn't go deep-sea diving without at least some basic knowledge, you can't start pooing at work like a pro without preparation. We will therefore begin with basic concepts that you should already know. Unfortunately, you do not know them because there is a total lack of training on this subject in UK companies.

HOW TO POO AT WORK

You discover that the flush does not work

Although all employees must relieve themselves in the company bathroom, no training on pooing at work is ever offered. We know that a PowerPoint presentation like the illustration above has never taken place in your company. That is why we wrote this book.

In these pages you will discover that you have made mistakes when pooing at work, but don't dwell on your past slip-ups. By deciding to read this book you have made an important and life-changing decision. With its help, you will forever change the way you poo at work and with that, your entire career! This book will help you to make your way to the top. You will understand the pitfalls to avoid, and make those precious first steps towards promotion. Anything will be possible if you just make that effort.

We won't lie — the road ahead is long and sometimes difficult. But you now have two trustworthy and knowledgeable coaches who will guide you through all the toilet conundrums you'll ever encounter in your career. Your toilet trips will soon no longer be an obstacle to the career you deserve.

To keep this promise we have chosen an original approach to give you solutions to every toilet dilemma. We will tackle all situations, even the really tricky ones and we will finally reveal the golden rules of the workplace bathroom.

"Don't let a number 2 stop you from being number 1 on the job!"

Tom Hayatt

THE GOLDEN RULES

The toilets at the workplace are governed by six clear rules. Even if they have never been written or formally defined, subconsciously everyone follows these rules. You can never break them, whatever the situation.

Rule 1:   Never make eye contact with another person in the toilet

Rule 2:   Never start a conversation with another person in the toilet

Rule 3:   Create maximum distance between you and other persons present in the toilet

Rule 4:   Never express what you feel inside

Rule 5:   Stay impassive, no matter what may have happened in the toilet

Rule 6:   Never make excuses in an effort to minimize attention to an event

THE SIX N-RULES

Tom Hayatt, the indisputable authority on the subject of toilets in the work-place, has compiled these rules under the title 'The Six N-Rules'.

1. No Eye Contact   **4.** No Emotion
2. No Talking   **5.** Not Guilty
3. No Contact   **6.** No Excuses

Another Golden Rule

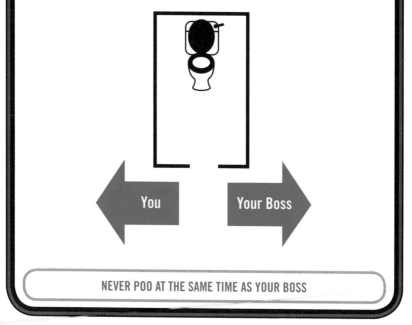

NEVER POO AT THE SAME TIME AS YOUR BOSS

TEST YOURSELF!

1. What does the acronym TML3S invented by Tom Hayatt stand for?
2. What are 'The Six N-Rules'?
3. What are the essential ingredients that will ensure success in your career?

Once you have answered these three questions, you will be ready to study the revolutionary 'Circular Look' method.

"What is the recipe for successful achievement?
To my mind there are just four essential ingredients:

1. Choose a career you love.

2. Give it your very best.

3. Seize your opportunities.

4. Be good at pooing at work.

I believe you are one of the people who are able to
fulfil all four of these requirements."

Tom Hayatt

AS SOON AS YOU ENTER THE STALL...

We have invented a special process that will help you whenever you need to poo at work. Carefully tested in the field for ten years, this method will enable you to poo at work with minimal risk. It is of crucial importance that you apply this process prior to each poo.

A thorough check of the stall will enable you to see if it is adapted to what you need to do in there. Even after years of pooing at work using our methods, keep in mind that dangers lurk everywhere and no pooer, expert or beginner, will avoid them if he or she doesn't respect this process. Never get overconfident about pooing at work!

When you enter a stall, you need to verify four points as quickly as possible. By practising and perfecting the 'Circular Look' method invented by Tom Hayatt, you should be able to check these four points in less than a second.

Here are the four things to check as soon as you enter the stall:

1. Is the toilet blocked?
2. Is the seat dirty?
3. Is there enough toilet paper?
4. Is the flush working?

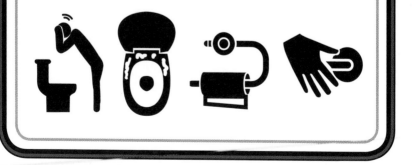

LEAVE THE DOOR OPEN WHILE CHECKING!

If you close the door and then open it 10 or 20 seconds later because of a problem you did not anticipate, anyone who has just entered the bathroom will think that you created the issue in the stall. If you want to get promoted, you do not want to be perceived as:

- The employee who blocked the toilet
- The employee who pees on the toilet seat
- The employee who uses a lot of toilet paper and leaves the dispenser empty
- The employee who broke the flush

So leave the door of the stall open and if you see anything wrong in the toilet, get out – quickly!

To do this check as quickly as possible, use Tom Hayatt's tips and his order of verification.

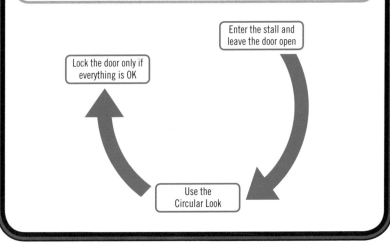

Enter the stall and leave the door open

Use the Circular Look

Lock the door only if everything is OK

Train yourself to be good at this check. In a couple of months, you must be able to check all four points in less than one second.

"If you want to ensure career advancement, get better at pooing at work."

Tom Hayatt

check that the toilet is not dirty

check that there is enough toilet paper

check that the flush is working

check that the toilet is not blocked

Is the cubicle ready for take-off? The Circular Look

Very important: When you do the check, leave the door open!

THE BEST POSITION TO POO IN A STALL!

Pooing at work is not easy. Abandoning the comfy toilets of our homes for cold cubicles with thin walls is a real challenge. Even employees who like to face challenges at work do not like this one. Pooing at work is always a source of anxiety because workplace toilets tend to be full of surprises. And it is quite understandable if, under such stressful conditions, you just can't do the deed.

At work you are already under a lot of pressure and it can be difficult to relax your sphincter. As you are not as comfortable as you would be at home, we recommend you do not to use the 'Thinker Position' (illustrated). If you do so, you may have difficulties unloading because this position blocks your flow. Tom Hayatt recommends you look up 'kinked colon' on Google.

Instead, try this new position which will massively improve your workplace poo! You will be more relaxed and your colon will be in natural alignment.

Warning

In this position, if you need to push hard (which happens to all of us) you must be careful not to break the door with your feet. This happened a couple of times when we tested the position at our publisher's office.

You will be encouraged to know that many readers of this book who previously worked from home in fear of the more rudimentary workplace toilets are now completely relaxed when they poo at work. Try it!

TOM HAYATT'S OPINION

There is a second good reason to use this technique. In a bathroom at work, the stall door always has a gap at the bottom that ordinarily facilitates access to the cleaning staff. It also makes your shoes visible and exposes you to the danger of being recognized by those who might walk into the toilet. If you use this method, people cannot see your shoes and cannot know that you are pushing inside this cubicle.

HOW TO GO TO THE BATHROOM

To guarantee safe visits to the toilet, without any danger to your career, you must have a plan. 99% of employees don't have a plan. They feel the urge to poo and just go to the bathroom as quickly as they can. Some of them are spotted by their boss, trying to run down a corridor with clenched buttocks. If want to get promoted, you don't want to get noticed for that kind of thing. We have made two very simple diagrams so you do not make two very simple mistakes.

"Pooing at work is easy if you do what's right, the right way at the right time."

Tom Hayatt

"When you poo at work, patience is the first rule of success!"

William Feather

TIPS TO LOOK EFFICIENT

Send emails from the toilet

Can you log in to your work email from the toilet? Perfect. Take to replying to emails at times when you are in there so people will not know you are in there. Just don't overdo it or you'll risk looking like an employee who is sending emails from the toilet. A good trick here is to have a series of emails ready to send. Then, when you're safely at 'Mr Brown's desk', you can hit send and spend some quality time researching something more interesting.

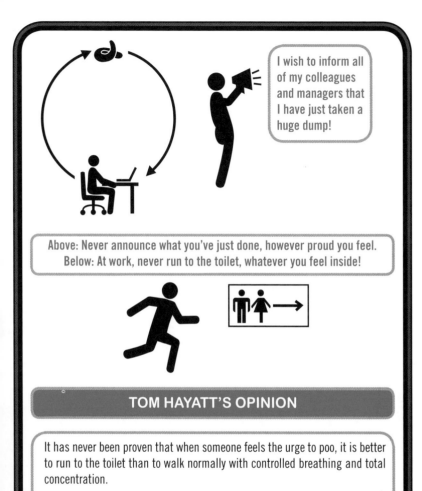

Above: Never announce what you've just done, however proud you feel.
Below: At work, never run to the toilet, whatever you feel inside!

TOM HAYATT'S OPINION

It has never been proven that when someone feels the urge to poo, it is better to run to the toilet than to walk normally with controlled breathing and total concentration.

All human beings face two dilemmas in life:

1. To reach shelter from the rain, should you dash recklessly over slippery ground or walk serenely under the downpour?
2. When feeling the urge to poo, should you run to the bathroom and disturb your inner tranquillity or walk with calm dignity?

BASIC SKILLS

The coffee trick

1. Work at your desk.
2. Walk slowly to the bathroom.
3. Try to do your deed as quickly as possible without getting noticed and without making noise.
4. Go to the coffee machine.
5. Come back to your desk with your coffee in hand. Drink your coffee at your desk and look around. It is a way to tell everyone that you went for a coffee and not for a massive poo.

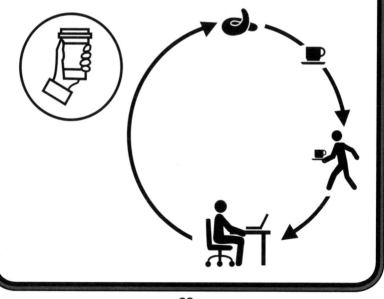

The photocopier trick

1. Work at your desk.
2. Take a folder and some paper to make other employees believe that you are going to the photocopier.
3. Walk slowly to the bathroom.
4. Do your deed as quickly as possible without getting noticed and without making noise.
5. Come back to your desk with your folder. Everybody will believe that you are doing important work for the company.

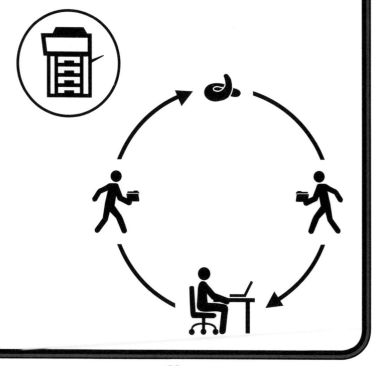

BASIC SKILLS

The safest trick

For a very safe trip, you can combine techniques.

1. Work at your desk.
2. Take a folder and some paper to make other employees believe that you are going to the photocopier to do important work for the company.
3. Walk slowly to the bathroom.
4. Do your deed as quickly as possible without getting noticed and without making noise.
5. Go to the coffee machine.
6. Come back to your desk with your folder and a coffee. Say hello to as many people as you can in the corridor so everybody knows that you went for a coffee and a copy and not for a poo.

HOW TO MAKE YOUR OWN POO AT WORK LOG

You want to make real progress in pooing at work? Our expert Tom Hayatt strongly believes that every employee should create and keep their own 'Poo at Work' log. It is a must for anyone serious about their career. Don't look for one in stores as, unfortunately, they don't exist (yet). Tom Hayatt suggests you ask for a notebook from your work's stationery supplier and use it to keep track of all your workplace poos over time. This workbook is like having a personal poo coach. It will benefit you tremendously and will help you to poo.

Creating your own poo log is quite simple and takes only a few minutes. On top of basic information like the date and time, you can customize it according to your wishes and objectives. In one year, it will be a must read if you wish to gain a deeper understanding of your workplace pooing (timing, size, challenges...) and take your poos to the next level.

"Having your own poo log is indispensable if you want to make progress in your workplace poo techniques."

Tom Hayatt

CHAPTER 2

Common problems encountered when going to a workplace toilet

In this chapter, you will find solutions to the most common problems that employees encounter when going to the workplace toilet. We are going to tackle them, one by one, and suggest concrete, proven solutions.

"The loudest one in the boardroom is the strongest one in the boardroom. The loudest one in the bathroom is the weakest one in the bathroom."

Tom Hayatt

The dangers

Every problem in this chapter is inspired by real events. The key below will help identify potential pitfalls with the following problematic scenarios.

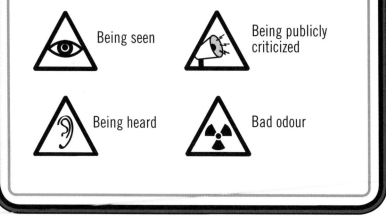

Being seen

Being publicly criticized

Being heard

Bad odour

You are in a meeting with your boss and colleagues. You switched off your mobile phone at the request of your boss, who does not want anything to disturb the meeting. Although you have been trying to resist for a long time, it becomes imperative that you go to the toilet.

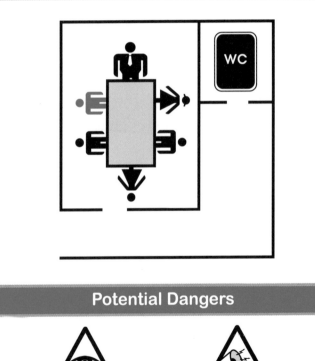

Potential Dangers

SOLUTION: The Four Winds

1. Pick the quietest and most reserved colleague at the table (let's call him 'Paul').

2. Simulate loud flatulence while continuing to concentrate on the discussion.

3. Simulate flatulence again. Give your target a suspicious stare.

4. Simulate flatulence for the third time. Get up while exclaiming: "For heaven's sake, Paul, are you done? We're in a meeting!"

5. Do not flinch at your boss's stare or your victim's protests.

6. Raise your voice and say: "Are you suggesting it was the boss?"

7. Sit down and simulate one last flatulence.

8. Storm out, yelling: "What an animal! I'll come back after you've ventilated the room."

9. Once you return from the bathroom, re-enter haughtily, with: "OK, I'll come back, but Paul, restrain yourself this time. Can we now get back to work? Where were we?"

Difficulty

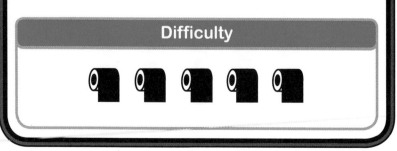

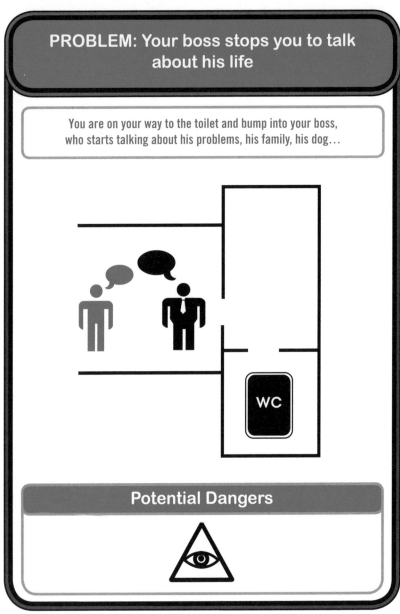

PROBLEM: Your boss stops you to talk about his life

You are on your way to the toilet and bump into your boss, who starts talking about his problems, his family, his dog…

WC

Potential Dangers

1. Don't show what you're feeling inside. Don't cross your legs or hold your buttocks together.

2. Pretend that what he is saying interests you. Nod and occasionally say: "Mm, yes of course, indeed, you are right."

3. Then change the subject to your work.

4. Ask for a 30% pay rise. This will make your boss come up with an excuse, like an important meeting he is already late for, and he will leave you alone.

Difficulty

PROBLEM: Your boss enters at the same time as you

You are on your way to the toilets. The moment you get to the door, your boss appears and enters the room with you.

Potential Dangers

SOLUTION: The Abort Mission!

1. Keep your cool and remember one of the golden rules: don't talk to him. The situation is not as desperate as it seems. Don't forget that your boss also feels uncomfortable.

2. Walk briskly and assuredly towards the basin. You want to make him think that you only came in to wash your hands.

3. Wash your hands and let the water run to make as much noise as possible.

4. Start the hand dryer.

5. Leave by closing the door loudly. That way your boss will know that you have left and will be grateful to do his business in peace.

Difficulty

PROBLEM: The toilet is overflowing

You are in the toilet and have just finished. When you flush,
the water keeps rising and finally overflows. In this kind of scenario,
you have only a fraction of a second to act.

Potential Dangers

SOLUTION: Noah's Ark

1. As soon as you see that overflow is inevitable, close the lid.

2. Quickly climb on top of the toilet.

3. Grab the toilet brush and as much toilet paper as you can.

4. Throw the paper all over the floor. It will absorb the water. Then use the toilet brush to gather the wet paper into a pile.

5. Once the floor is dry enough, step off the toilet.

6. Anonymously call maintenance and let them know that 'Paul' has blocked the toilet again.

Difficulty

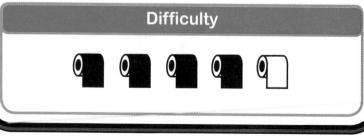

PROBLEM: The toilet paper roll escapes from the stall

You are sitting on the toilet. The roll of toilet paper that you are using drops to the floor and rolls out of the cubicle.

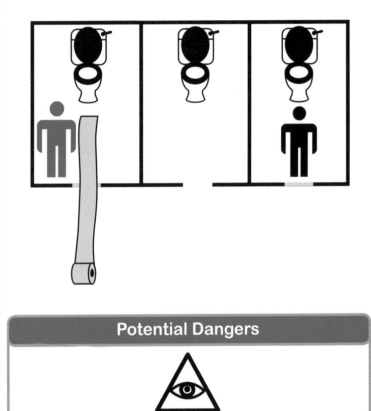

Potential Dangers

SOLUTION: Ariadne's Thread

1. Forget about the idiotic method of pulling the paper towards you, which will only make it roll further and further away.

2. Discreetly grab hold of the end of the roll that is still in your stall.

3. Slowly slide it under the wall into the stall next to yours, making it seem that it is coming out of there.

4. Leave your stall as if nothing happened.

Difficulty

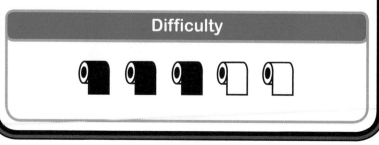

You walk into a toilet stall and you notice that the door doesn't lock. You can't leave.

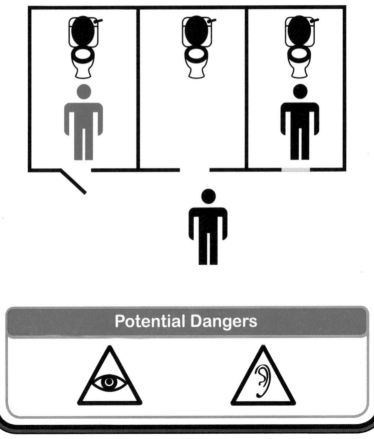

Potential Dangers

SOLUTION: Embrace the Fear

1. Close the door.

2. Sit and try to poo.

3. You will have some difficulty pooing because you are nervous that someone might open the door and see... everything.

4. It is one of the biggest challenges you can face in a cubicle. You must relax to be able to poo but also be ready to throw yourself at the door if anyone tries to open it. If this happens, don't scream "Occupied!". People might recognize your voice and that would not benefit your career.

Difficulty

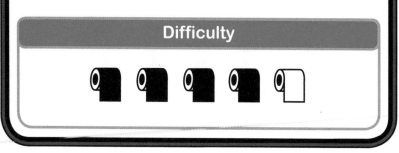

PROBLEM: Your boss must be in the next stall

Your boss wasn't in his office. You enter the toilets and you just know that he is in one of the occupied stalls.

Potential Dangers

1. Just after you enter the room, turn off the light.

2. You should then hear: "Hey, the light!"

3. Turn on the light.

4. If you think you recognized the voice of your boss, turn the light off again to double-check.

5. You should hear from the stall: "The light, damn it!"

6. If it is indeed your boss, leave the place immediately (turning on the light or not, depending on the level of affinity you have with him and if you have been promoted recently or not).

7. Come back to the toilet once he has left.

Difficulty

PROBLEM: There is no paper in your stall

You are in a busy toilet with several stalls and you suddenly realize that yours has no toilet paper. There is probably some in the next stall, but if you leave yours and go into another one, you'll look ridiculous.

Potential Dangers

SOLUTION: The Stocktaker

1. Find out if anyone is in the stall on the left by throwing some water over the wall. If an annoyed "Heeey!" comes from it, it means that someone is in this stall. Repeat the tactic for the stall on the right.

2. Slide your hand under the separation with the empty stall.

3. Feel along the wall with your hand and try catching the end of the toilet paper roll there.

4. Take a sufficient amount of toilet paper.

5. Finally, do what you came in to do.

Difficulty

PROBLEM: There is not enough paper

You have just finished and pull on the paper dispenser,
only to find that just three measly leaves remain.
You forgot the 'Circular Look' method, shame on you!

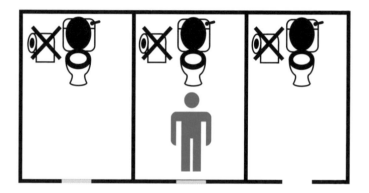

Potential Dangers

SOLUTION: The Rough Ride

1. Don't call out for someone to bring you more toilet paper. You are at work, not at home.

2. Pray to all the gods whose names you remember that you have a packet of tissues in your pocket. Unfortunately, the gods find this kind of thing funny and will probably do nothing.

3. Take the toilet paper distributor apart.

4. Pick up the empty toilet roll.

5. With your nails, cut off strips of cardboard, making them as thin as possible.

6. Use this as toilet paper. Be careful not to make the strips too thick or you may risk blocking the toilet.

Difficulty

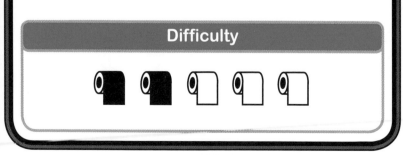

PROBLEM: You are constipated and somebody knocks on the door insistently

You are in a toilet stall with separating walls. Suddenly, you see the shadow of a person outside who is visibly in a hurry, pacing in front of your door. This person knocks on your door insistently, even though the lock clearly indicates that your stall is occupied.

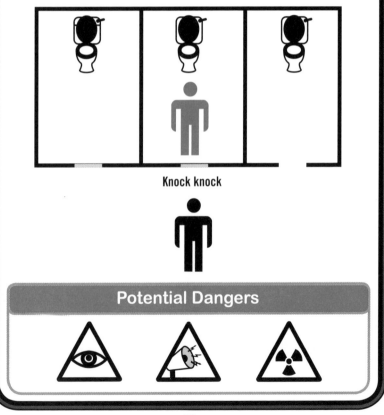

Knock knock

Potential Dangers

SOLUTION: The Brush-off

1. Carefully observe the shadow of the impatient person and his movements. You should then be able to anticipate his next approach and knock.

2. Approach your door in silence.

3. Grab the toilet brush.

4. When the person outside is about to knock, slide your hand under the door.

5. With a quick movement, swipe the toilet brush over the shoes and possibly the trousers of the person outside.

6. The person outside will be shocked and annoyed, but will never knock on your door again.

Difficulty

PROBLEM: You make too much noise

You are seated on the toilet. A repeated 'splash' risks alerting other people in the room to your presence – and what you are doing.

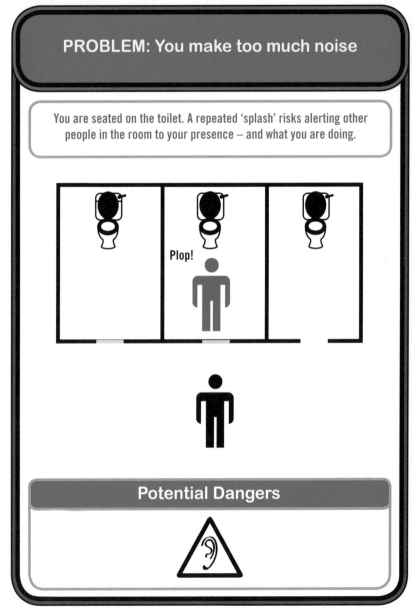

Potential Dangers

SOLUTION: The Landing Cushion

1. Before sitting down, tear off a few pieces of toilet paper.

2. Throw them into the toilet bowl in a way that will provide efficient soundproofing.

3. You can now attend to your business without worrying.

> *"The top people of the biggest companies are, surprisingly, often the best at pooing in their company. You can be sure that they got there because they worked hard and were good at pooing at work."*
>
> Tom Hayatt

Difficulty

PROBLEM: Someone turns off the light

Just after you enter the stall and sit down to business, someone turns off the light.

Potential Dangers

1. Do not scream at the top of your voice "The light, damn it! I am pooing and I am not finished yet!"

2. Don't panic, you can make it! You have probably gone through the motions more than 1,000 times in this cubicle because — like everybody — you always go to the same cubicle when you poo at work.

3. Finish your poo. The dark will actually help you relax. In one short minute, you will feel much relieved.

4. Visualize the toilet paper dispenser and how it works. Go for it, you do not need to see it, your hand will find it naturally.

5. Stand up and flush.

6. Now, the tricky part. Look for the handle of the toilet brush. Brush the toilet bowl in the dark. Brush everywhere else too as you do not know where it is dirty and if it is dirty.

7. Don't go out immediately. Listen. Find the lock with your hand and go out if you are quite sure that nobody will be coming into the bathroom. You do not want to come across your boss, as he would immediately realize that you just pooed in the dark. And although he would be impressed by this skill he wouldn't be impressed that you were caught brown-handed, so to speak.

Difficulty

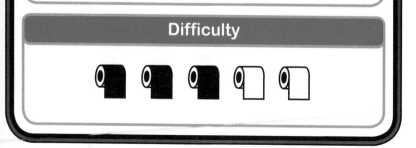

51

10 alternatives to toilet paper that can be found in the workplace

Unfortunately, it often happens that there is no toilet paper in any of the workplace cubicles. Why? Because when there is no paper in one cubicle, employees simply move on to the next until the supply is exhausted. Of course no one notifies the stationery department because that would be an admission of pooing.

When there is no toilet paper or not enough toilet paper, you won't find a solution later, just after your poo. The priority is not the one your body is telling you. You must find a solution before!

Here are 10 things that you can use instead of toilet paper.

1. Bubble wrap

Expert opinion: Be gentle so that you don't pop the bubbles.

2. Tinfoil

Expert opinion: Careful, this tears easily. Use at least three layers. You can find it in the shared fridge around the sandwich of an employee.

3. Bread

Expert opinion: Can be found at the canteen. Opt for fresh bread rather than toasted

4. Cardboard

Expert opinion: Difficult to handle and painful during use. I would not recommend it.

5. Newspaper

Expert opinion: Be careful, the business paper with the pink pages can give you a colourful bum.

6. Tree leaves

Expert opinion: You will need to go out of the office. Doesn't work with spruce tree.

7. A supermarket plastic bag

Expert opinion: Very practical: it protects the whole hand.

8. Socks

Expert opinion: Be careful because as the saying goes: Socks with holes, hands with moles.

9. A towel

Expert opinion: If you do not have one, try to steal the towel of an employee who goes to the gym after work.

10. A dishwashing sponge

Expert opinion: Never use the side intended for scrubbing.

CHAPTER THREE

Pooing during business trips and outdoor team building

Travelling abroad on business is a real challenge because pooing in strange toilets is unavoidable. Normally when you can't face going at work, you can wait until evening to poo in your comfy toilet at home. But on a business trip, waiting days to get back home and poo is not an option.

The increase in business travel calls for a chapter on the toilet customs and traditions of faraway lands and ways to avoid Business Trip Poo Syndrome (inability to do your deed when away from home). If you travel on business, you certainly wouldn't want your boss to bring together the whole team and announce, "Guys, I have bad news. Paul will be heading home early because he hasn't been able to poo since the beginning of the trip. An emergency medical team will evacuate him back to the UK today."

Some people might recommend that you avoid long-haul business trips altogether, but we know that they are often essential to your career. If you want to make your way to the top, you need to be able to poo confidently during your travels.

Human civilization has provided a source of endless wonder when it comes to the diverse methods of dealing with human waste. A good example is the Japanese toilet; its elaborate technology can be hazardous to those not familiar with it – a cleansing water jet mistakenly set to a temperature of 95 degrees… burns. As for the more exotic countries where the best business opportunities can be found, you would be understandably terrified if you knew what awaited you in their toilets. What do you do when you find yourself stuck in a ramshackle toilet whose lock hasn't been oiled in 15 years and your boss is waiting for you in the meeting room?

EXPERT ADVICE

When you travel to an exotic country on a business trip, do your best to do a first poo when you land at the airport. This will often be your last chance to use a comfortable bathroom. An opportunity you will not want to pass up, believe me.

WARNING

When abroad, don't look for new business opportunities in the toilets! Whatever the country, keep in mind that toilets in the workplace are governed by the same six rules. You can never break them, whatever the situation or the nation. Somebody entering the toilets will never be open to closing a deal with you, he has something else in mind. However, toilets are small spaces that facilitate new encounters, as long as you keep them casual. Start a conversation only with a businessman who is washing his hands and has obviously finished his other business.

PROBLEM: You are on a business trip in an exotic country

You are on a business trip to a subsidiary in another country and have no idea what rules are in place regarding the use of company toilets. Also, you don't know if 'Toskityskitze' means 'Gents'. It could very well be that what you take for the men's toilet is, in fact, the ladies' toilet, or something else entirely.

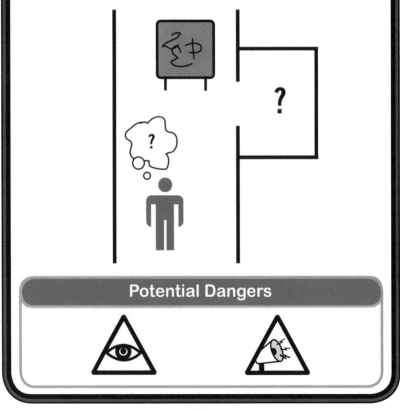

Potential Dangers

SOLUTION: The Trojan Horse

1. Do not ask your business partner for an explanation. You do not want him to bring your entire team to the bathroom for training and, in the days to come, to be asked if you managed to poo each time you come back from there. He might also give you additional poo-related advice during your stay. Trust us, you do not want to hear it.

2. The key point is not to wait until you feel the urge to poo. As soon as you get to the building, locate the possible toilet.

3. Walk regularly in front of the supposed toilet and try to see what people are doing inside. Make a note of their comings and goings. Do they stay for five minutes or longer? Do they seem happier and more relaxed when they leave this room?

4. As soon as you are certain that this is the bathroom and that the room is empty, enter the toilet and try to understand how things work. Try to gather as much information as possible to be 100% ready for when you have to do your business in there.

5. Leave this country as soon as possible.

Difficulty

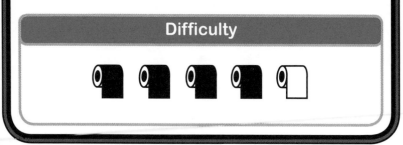

PROBLEM: You are in Japan, faced with a high-tech toilet

A few hours after arriving in Japan, a strong urge comes over you. For the first time in your life you will have to use a toilet that is more sophisticated than the one back home. When facing any new system, caution is always the best policy.

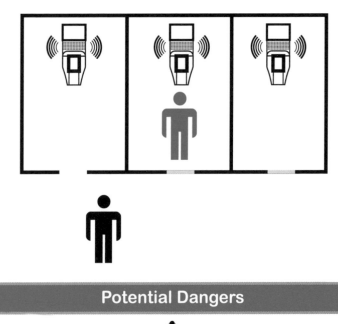

Potential Dangers

SOLUTION: The Hit and Run

1. Do not ask anyone for help; in Japanese culture, asking for help when going to the toilet is considered an insult. You will have to figure it out on your own!

2. Approach the toilet and remove any necessary items of clothing. Avoid touching the seat – it may have sensors linked to the flushing mechanism.

3. Sit down, do what you came to do as gently as possible and get dressed.

4. Once finished, do not flush: open the door of your stall first.

5. Close your eyes, cover up your face with your hands and quickly press all of the buttons simultaneously.

6. Run as fast as you can to leave the toilets and find a safe zone.

7. On the way, do not look back no matter what happens, and never stop, whatever may be going on behind you.

8. Take your hands from your face only when you have reached your safe zone.

Difficulty

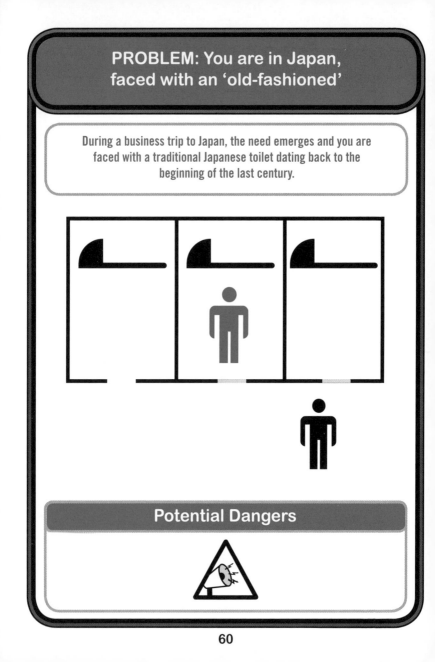

SOLUTION: Riding a Bike

1. Be aware, these toilets are culturally significant. Respect them.

2. Position yourself as if you were mounting a motorbike (the thicker part of the toilet should be in front).

3. Bend your knees to lower yourself over the pot.

4. Do your deed.

5. Wipe off while maintaining your balance. Tourists often find themselves falling backwards!

6. Flush.

Difficulty

PROBLEM: You are in Turkey, faced with a squat toilet

You are in Turkey where they only have squat toilets – also known in some countries as Turkish toilets. These perilous toilets require some prior knowledge on their safe use.

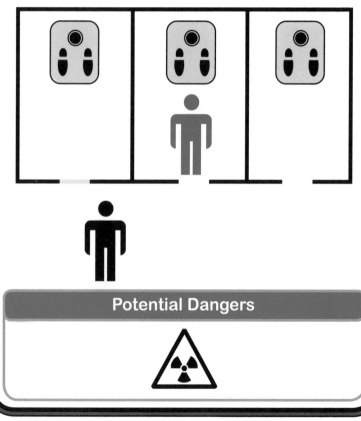

Potential Dangers

SOLUTION: Softly Softly

1. Do not go in there unless you really need to go. It's way too risky!

2. Face the door and place your feet on the two steps either side of the hole, with your bum directly over it.

3. Lower your trousers, but not too low as they may touch the toilet.

4. Carefully do your deed, always keeping in mind that you may get still get soiled.

5. Open the door, flush and run. The flush is almost always badly aligned and may cause polluted splashback or flooding.

Difficulty

PROBLEM: You are in Sweden faced with ecological toilets

Ecological toilets are often installed in workplaces in Sweden. You are faced with an Earth-friendly toilet and must be environmentally aware.

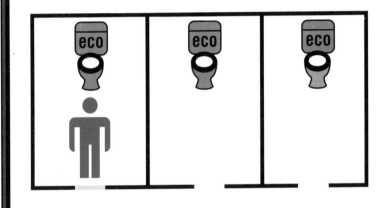

Potential Dangers

SOLUTION: Nature's Bounty

1. Enter the toilet stall made from wood that was transported on the back of an ethically sourced donkey.

2. Draw the Fairtrade organic cotton curtain.

3. Lower yourself onto the seat of unpolished wood and be careful not to get splinters in your bum.

4. Do your deed as usual, even if the smell makes you feel as if you are pooping in a sauna.

5. When finished, take a shovelful of sawdust and throw it over the heap in the hole under your seat.

6. Wipe yourself with the promotional leaflets that you were asked to bring along (now you know why).

7. Before going out, disinfect the seat with lemon slices that you will find in a cup beside the toilet.

Difficulty

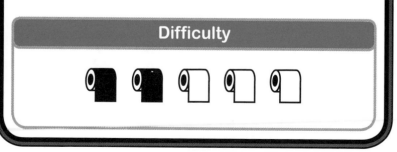

PROBLEM: You are sharing a hotel room with your boss

Like all companies in the UK, your company is trying to save money. For your business trip, only one room with twin beds has been booked. You share the room and the bathroom with your boss. After a hard day at work, you feel the urge to poo!

HOTEL ROOM

Potential Dangers

1. Do not even think of using the toilet inside your hotel room. The walls are always paper thin and your boss will hear every sound you make while doing your business: every echoing fart and every 'plop' that hits the water. He will hear you wiping your bottom and listen to make sure you wash your hands. He will picture you pooing and you really do not want that. He might even want a shower after you've unburdened yourself and will not appreciate the aroma you've left behind.

2. Here's what you need to do. Go outside and find the communal bathroom. Always poo in there and pray that your boss does the same, so you don't have to picture him pooing 2 metres from your bed.

Difficulty

PROBLEM: You need to poo during an outdoor team-building exercise

Your manager, like all other managers in the UK, wants his employees to work well together and be more productive. So he's decided to spend money on a day of outdoor team-building activities. After 6 hours of silly tasks, you feel the urge to poo.

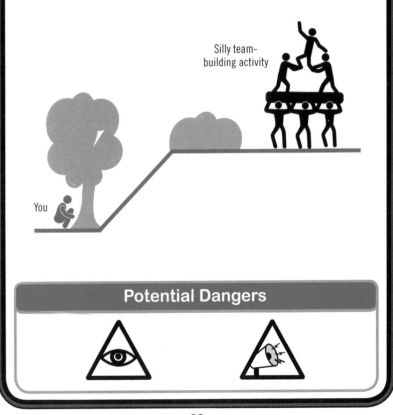

Silly team-building activity

You

Potential Dangers

We will give you three tips from our book *How to Poo in the Woods*:

1. Lowering your centre of gravity gives you excellent stability, even on an incline. The intestine is in the ideal natural position; the one that evolution has intended for pooping purposes.

2. Poo next to a tree, the trunk will allow you to support yourself and avoid falling.

3 Under no circumstances should you wait until the last moment to find something to wipe yourself with. Short-sighted employees will find themselves shuffling around the forest half-naked, like insane penguins searching for something, anything, to wipe themselves with, and could even meet their boss. Never take shortcuts with the golden rule of pooing outdoors. Even when you are about to explode, you must take the time to gather enough wiping material before unleashing the accumulated pressure on your intestines.

Difficulty

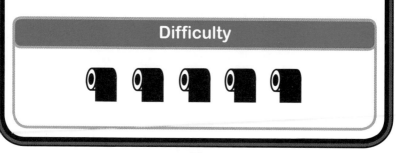

CHAPTER FOUR

How to fart at work

You now know that companies are governed by strict rules of conduct. Consequently, emitting a loud, smelly fart is never a good thing to do at work. Farting during a meeting or PowerPoint presentation is not following your company's best practice guidelines.

Before we begin this new chapter, we should say that the proper title ought to be 'How not to fart at work' or 'How to hold in a fart at work' or 'How to avoid getting blamed for farts at work'.

FART FACTS

Let's start with the numbers. Every employee farts on average 8 to 15 times a day in his workplace.

Everyone farts quietly in the office and nobody talks about it. Yet the evidence is everywhere:

- A colleague comes out of the lift and seems unhappy to see you. When you enter the lift, you find that it smells bad.
- A teammate jumps from his seat to attend to something important but only a minute later returns to his desk empty-handed.
- Your boss starts talking to you, then begins to fidget and leaves hastily.

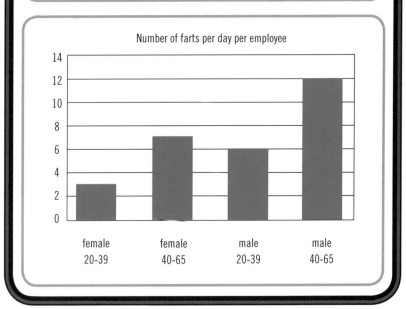

Number of farts per day per employee

We bet that in your workplace, no one has dared to tackle the issue. Did a manager organize a one-hour meeting with his team to discuss the problem of farts to try to find solutions all together? No. Have you ever had a farting brainstorm? No. Have you received an email outlining guidelines or best practices on farts at work? No. Did anyone think to put air freshener in the corner of the lift? No. Is there a soundproofed and ventilated room in your workplace for farting, just as there is for smoking? No. In your workplace as in so many others, the problem of farts is totally overlooked.

We have made some annual calculations with Excel to help understand the magnitude of the problem. An English company employs an average of 154 employees. Between 1,232 and 2,310 farts are released each day in a company. That's an average. In larger companies, it may exceed 30,000 farts and can go up to 50,000 farts per day when beans are served in the canteen.

In addition to the ventilation problem in most offices, there are thousands of situations where an employee needs to break wind in a hurry. This is a major source of stress, as one moment of inattention or poor estimation of path, noise or smell will reduce a successful career to zero. We all know what is at stake here. You only need to get caught twice to be nicknamed 'Mr Fartypants' and become the colleague we all laugh at when he's not around, the employee with whom we do not eat in the canteen, the employee who will never be promoted...

We are working seriously to create solutions to problems in business that everyone pretends to ignore. It is important to us that careers are not reduced to zero because of a business lunch at the Mexican restaurant that led to gastroenteritis and a flatulence that was not as quiet as expected. To create this chapter, we spent 145 days in different companies to test and invent new techniques for farting at work. As with our other books, we were surrounded by a legion of experts, including gastroenterologists and specialists in aerodynamics.

From our research you will gain unparalleled knowledge in this complex area which combines medicine, chemistry and physics. You will know what to do after inadvertently breaking wind in a lift or even in the boss's office. You will understand the complex aerial phenomena of flatulence. You will choose your meals in the company canteen more carefully...

WHERE AND HOW TO FART AT WORK: 3 FACTORS

To successfully break wind at work, you must choose the right place and the right time.

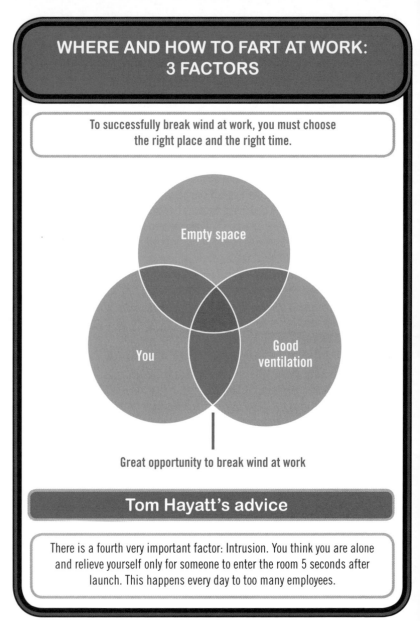

Great opportunity to break wind at work

Tom Hayatt's advice

There is a fourth very important factor: Intrusion. You think you are alone and relieve yourself only for someone to enter the room 5 seconds after launch. This happens every day to too many employees.

The PCF method

We recommend that you do not immediately release the fart as soon as you feel it brewing. When possible, use the PCF method: Plan - Check – Fart.

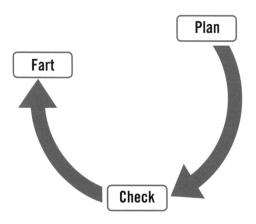

You're at work and you feel the urge to pass gas. Using the PCF method…

1. Offer to run for coffee or snacks so you can fart in peace on the way.
2. Pretend to respond to an email that calls you away.
3. Ask for some privacy to take a call.
4. Make a loud noise to cover the fart (for instance, cough loudly).

WHERE TO FART

Step 1: Go quickly to the nearest safe space

The two best places to fart are a cubicle in the toilets or on the fire escape.

Step 2: Keep calm and fart in peace

Use one of these very efficient positions.

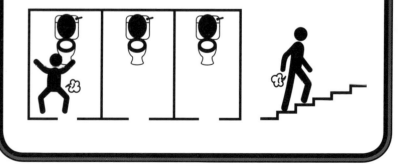

Two tips when you're at lunch

Employees who fart less tend to avoid eating or drinking too fast. They also eat less of the foods that cause flatulence. It's as simple as that. Do the same.

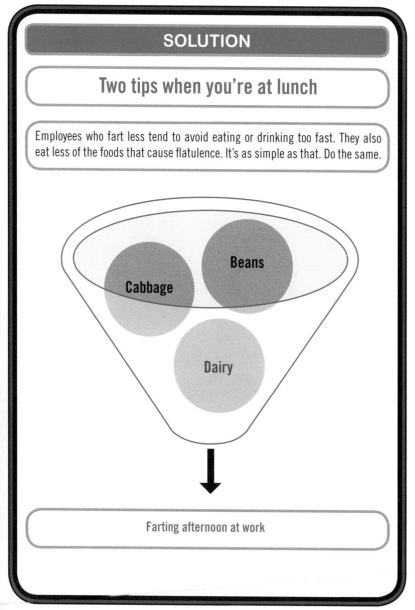

Beans

Cabbage

Dairy

Farting afternoon at work

HOW TO BREAK WIND IN YOUR OFFICE

If this question seems simple to you, it means you have not thought enough about it and that you take risks.

For the launch, you have two choices:

1. Stay at your desk and lift your leg.   2. Move and lift your leg.

The second technique is the best because it is often less noisy. We also recommend that you think before acting. You should always anticipate that a person can come into your office the second after you launch. Consider farting in the corner of your office where nobody goes.

NEVER USE THESE SIX TECHNIQUES TO FART AT WORK!

Whether it's during a conversation at the coffee machine, in the corridor or standing in your office, you should never use any of the following techniques. Everybody knows them, and you'll be fooling no one.

PHYSICS MADE SIMPLE

Most employees' knowledge of flatulence is worryingly rudimentary. Many only know what their parents have taught them about this strange phenomenon.

The flatus gasses in the stomach are at the same temperature as the body. Therefore, they are warmer than the surrounding air. When they are launched, these gases follow the same laws of physics as any other gas: they rise up and that's why they get up to your nose.

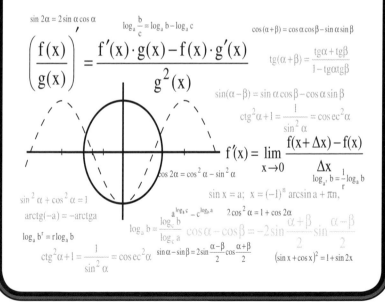

$$\sin 2\alpha = 2\sin\alpha\cos\alpha$$

$$\log_a \frac{b}{c} = \log_a b - \log_a c$$

$$\cos(\alpha+\beta) = \cos\alpha\cos\beta - \sin\alpha\sin\beta$$

$$\left(\frac{f(x)}{g(x)}\right)' = \frac{f'(x)\cdot g(x) - f(x)\cdot g'(x)}{g^2(x)}$$

$$\tg(\alpha+\beta) = \frac{\tg\alpha + \tg\beta}{1 - \tg\alpha\tg\beta}$$

$$\sin(\alpha-\beta) = \sin\alpha\cos\beta - \cos\alpha\sin\beta$$

$$\ctg^2\alpha + 1 = \frac{1}{\sin^2\alpha} = \cos ec^2\alpha$$

$$f'(x) = \lim_{x\to 0}\frac{f(x+\Delta x) - f(x)}{\Delta x}$$

$$\cos 2\alpha = \cos^2\alpha - \sin^2\alpha$$

$$\log_{a^r} b = \frac{1}{r}\log_a b$$

$$\sin x = a; \quad x = (-1)^n \arcsin a + \pi n,$$

$$\sin^2\alpha + \cos^2\alpha = 1$$

$$\arctg(-a) = -\arctg a$$

$$2\cos^2\alpha = 1 + \cos 2\alpha$$

$$\log_a b = \frac{\log_c b}{\log_c a}$$

$$a^{\log_b c} - c^{\log_b a}$$

$$\log_a b^r = r\log_a b$$

$$\cos\alpha - \cos\beta = -2\sin\frac{\alpha+\beta}{2}\sin\frac{\alpha-\beta}{2}$$

$$\ctg^2\alpha + 1 = \frac{1}{\sin^2\alpha} = \cos ec^2\alpha$$

$$\sin\alpha - \sin\beta = 2\sin\frac{\alpha-\beta}{2}\cos\frac{\alpha+\beta}{2}$$

$$(\sin x + \cos x)^2 = 1 + \sin 2x$$

80

Some simple physics

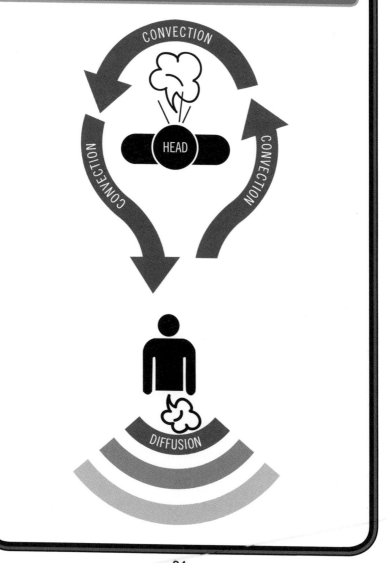

YOU BREAK WIND AT YOUR DESK. WHEN WILL THEY NOTICE THE SMELL?

You fart. You do not know how long it will be before your colleagues or boss notices it. Fortunately, there is a mathematical formula for that.

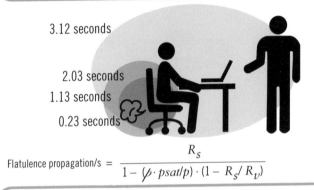

3.12 seconds

2.03 seconds

1.13 seconds

0.23 seconds

Flatulence propagation/s = $\dfrac{R_s}{1 - (\not{p} \cdot psat/p) \cdot (1 - R_s/R_v)}$

We would like to thank the Massachusetts Institute of Technology (MIT) for lending us its room with sensors so we could carry out our study of farts at work:

- If your colleague is in front of your desk, you have 3.12 seconds before he realizes you farted.
- If your colleague is behind you, you have 1.13 seconds before he realizes you farted.

This study obviously concerns a silent flatulence because if you make a noise, you should know that sound travels at 340.29 m/s and in this case, your colleague knows immediately. Hence the importance of training at home to release silent farts.

We advise you to always face your colleague because in the case of flatulence, you can use these valuable seconds to invite him to immediately leave your office.

YOU BREAK WIND IN A CORRIDOR OR AT THE COFFEE MACHINE

We conducted the same study and used the same formula to calculate the time you have before a group of interlocutors realize that you farted.

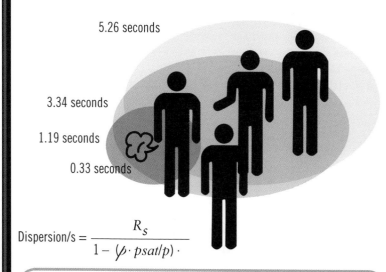

5.26 seconds

3.34 seconds

1.19 seconds

0.33 seconds

$$\text{Dispersion/s} = \frac{R_s}{1 - (\rho \cdot psat/p) \cdot}$$

In a group situation, where the issuer inadvertently lets loose a silent and smelly flatulence, he has only a short time before his colleagues (also referred to as receptors) understand what has just happened.

In this situation, in 3.34 seconds, two co-workers located less than 2 meters away are already overwhelmed by the smell. They possibly consider leaving the area.

HOW TO FART IN A LIFT AT WORK

We will now explain why you often feel the need to fart when the lift goes up and not when it comes down.

You have certainly noticed that you or your colleagues fart more often in the lift and that nobody knows how to handle this embarrassing situation. Due to a lack of scientific knowledge, most employees do not know why they fart more when they are in a lift. The reason is accessible to anyone who followed some of their physics lessons at school. With altitude, there is an air pressure change which must be rebalanced.

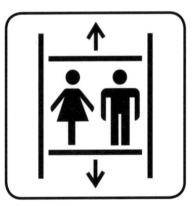

Did you know?

9% of farts in the workplace are made in lifts

YOU CAN FART IN A LIFT GOING UP

Once released, the fart air will head towards the floor of the lift. So, if the release is not loud, you can fart in a lift that goes up two or three times without any problem.

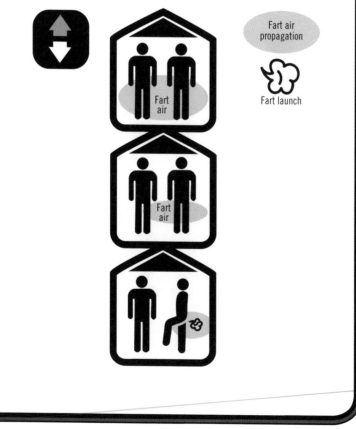

Fart air propagation

Fart launch

NEVER FART IN A LIFT GOING DOWN!

The fart air will gradually rise as the lift goes down and, some floors after release, the fart will be at nose level. Your fellow passengers will immediately realize what has happened, and seek out the guilty party. If there are only two of you in the lift, he will not be difficult to find...

Fart air propagation

Fart launch

Fart air

Fart air

WHEN CAN YOU FART SAFELY ON THE STAIRS?

If someone is following you down the stairs, do not fart! You must hold it in.

If you pass a colleague or the manager of the company on the stairs, you must wait at least two steps before you break wind (according to our tests).

Danger zone | Safety zone

PROBLEM: There is a horrible smell in the lift

You enter the elevator and you notice an awful odour left by a colleague. Or you were alone in the elevator, broke wind and now the smell is unbearable. How do you avoid suffocation?

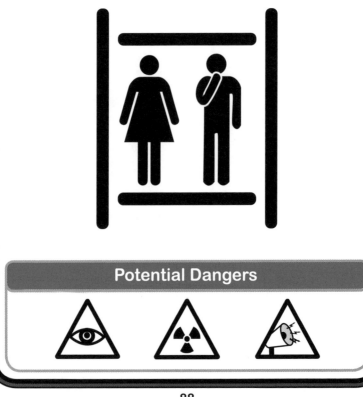

Potential Dangers

SOLUTION: The Deep-sea Diver

1. Pinch your nose.
2. Immediately press the button for the destination floor. Avoid delay, every second saved is important.
3. Press your mouth against the gap in doors and try to suck in some fresh air from outside.
4. Keep an eye on the dial that shows the floor to avoid being surprised by the doors opening. You may find yourself doing a duck face at your colleagues, or your boss who may be patiently waiting for the lift.

Difficulty

CHAPTER 5

How to discredit your colleagues and your boss

THE QUICKEST AND THE EASIEST PATH TO SUCCESS

You want to succeed in your job? You don't have tons of time for developmental seminars and you don't want to wait until the boss retires to get that promotion. A lot of books say that there is no easy path to success and that there is no route that skips the whole hard work part to get you there quickly. They even tell you that the journey is the fun part! All of this is bullshit to sell you books. Your job was to find the right book explaining the quick way to success and you've found it. You have found the simplest and best way to boost your career right now. Congratulations!

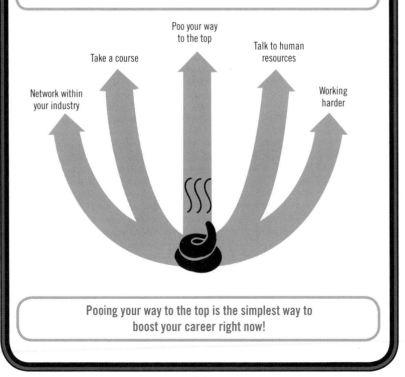

Network within your industry

Take a course

Poo your way to the top

Talk to human resources

Working harder

Pooing your way to the top is the simplest way to boost your career right now!

BASIC MID-TERM STRATEGY

You're on the fast track to success but, as you know, when you do things fast, things can get broken. Some of your colleagues and a couple of managers will suffer from your success. Accept it and don't worry about it. Nobody has ever made his way to the top without collateral damage. In this diagram, we show a simple strategy that you can implement at work in the coming year.

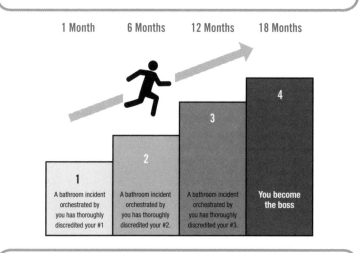

You must understand that, to poo your way to the top, you will have to discredit a colleague or even your boss. Many strategies are possible and we will present them in this chapter. They were developed by Tom Hayatt. Before using any of these techniques, you will always have to choose the colleague you wish to discredit. You need to think carefully and take the time to analyse your situation while consulting the company organization chart. We will help you make wise choices.

WHO SHOULD YOU DISCREDIT?

The first person you can target is your immediate boss, who we will refer to as #1, to try to take his place. Remember that you will need to discredit several people simultaneously. If you discredit your #1 and he is fired, it is important to have also discredited all employees who are eligible to take his place. The company boss, your #2 (#1's superior) and your #3 (#2's superior) must think that you are the only possible candidate available.

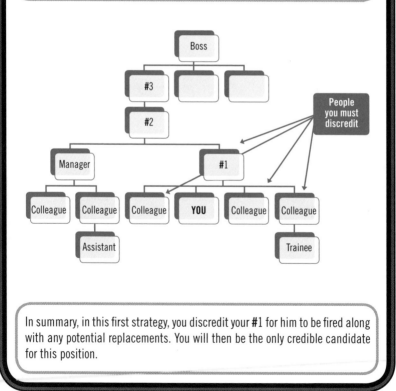

In summary, in this first strategy, you discredit your #1 for him to be fired along with any potential replacements. You will then be the only credible candidate for this position.

If you have a more altruistic personality, your #1 is not the best target. We recommend that you go straight for the boss of the company. The reason is obvious: if the boss is fired, many people will get promoted at the same time, including you.

If the boss is fired: #3 becomes the new boss; #2 becomes #3; #1 become #2; you become #1

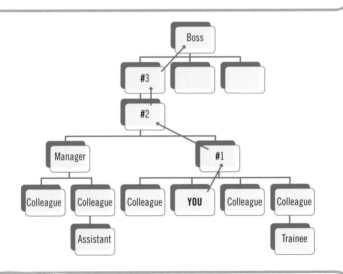

In some cases, you can even make an alliance to attack the boss together. Give this book to your #1, #2 and #3 and offer them a Machiavellian alliance to discredit the boss, using the techniques you discover in this chapter. Everyone will find benefit in the 'allied forces' because everyone will be promoted.

THINK OUTSIDE OF YOUR DEPARTMENT

You can also discredit the manager of another department and all the members of his team for good measure. You can then ask your #2 to recommend to the boss that you take the vacant position and bring your friends over into your new team.

What this flowchart clearly shows is that discrediting your own boss is not the only option available to you.

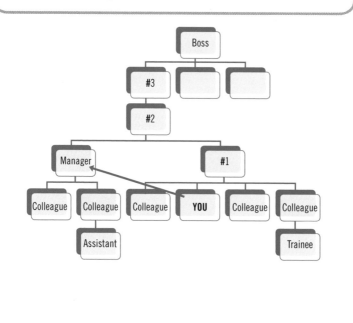

Optimum Safety Launch Window

To poo your way to the top, you will need an Excel file. Here is why: Have you ever noticed that your colleagues and your boss usually each go and do their business at the same time every day?

Almost all employees poo at the same time each day. Based on aeronautical science, we prepared the Safety Launch Window planning tool. Note when your colleagues, your #1, your #2 and the boss go to the toilet. With a little work, you will get to know your Optimum Safety Launch Window. With this you will be certain of never bumping into any of them in the bathroom. This is the first reason why you need the Excel table.

To prevent any incidents, never log your colleagues by their real names and store this page in a safe and inaccessible folder.

Colleague no	Nickname	06:00	07:00	08:00	09:00	10:00	11:00	12:00	13:00	14:00	15:00	16:00	17:00	18:00	19:00	20:00
Example	Stinky geeky			■												
1																
2																
3																
4																
5																
6																
7																
8																
9																
10																
BOSS																
My safety launch window																

Colleague no	Nickname	13:00	14:00	15:00	16:00	17:00	18:00	19:00	20:00
Example	Stinky geeky	■							
1									
2									
3									
4									
5									
6									
7									
8									
9									
10									
BOSS									
My safety launch window									

POO YOUR WAY TO THE TOP WITH 'OPTIMUM SAFETY LAUNCH WINDOW'

In this chapter, you will discover that knowing when your colleagues and bosses go to the toilet will help you to poo your way to the top. The data is invaluable for your career development. With our techniques, you will be able to use it against a colleague, your #1 or the boss of your company.

First, we will give you a very simple example of what you can do with the data:

If you know that your #1 goes to poo every day at about 10.05 a.m., at 09.50, you go to the bathroom with a screwdriver and lock all the doors from the outside. At 10.05, you #1 will be waiting in front of closed doors. At 10.10, he will begin to knock on one of them, then on each of them. At 10.20, he will be suffering. This powerful strategy is still a very basic one. With the Excel tool, you will soon discover that you can implement even better ones.

Just being a talented employee won't help your career. If there is someone who is better at pooing than you, he will get that promotion. If you can discredit this person, do it. End of story.

At work, it frequently happens that your colleague's boss asks you where they are. He often has an urgent question for him or is waiting for him to start a meeting. The question "Where is he?" is actually an opportunity. We will unveil a highly effective technique to gradually discredit any employee in the company.

Here's what you need to do:

If someone asks you where your colleague is, you should reply, "Paul? He's been in the toilet for half an hour" or "I think he went to the bathroom". Even if it isn't true. Here are some examples of what we advise you to do:

- If Paul is in a meeting and someone asks where he is, you answer "He's in the toilet".
- If Paul has gone for a smoke and someone asks where he is, you answer "He's in the toilet".
- If Paul went for a coffee and someone asks where he is, you answer "He's in the toilet".
- You get the idea.

REPLYING "He's in the toilet" is a technique that really works

Most people will be unable to avoid thinking of Paul sitting with his pants around his ankles or fumbling with the toilet paper dispenser. His image will be ever so slightly tarnished. All the time he has put into gaining respect over the years, all the money he invested in smart suits will be wasted if his #1 imagines him with those well-tailored trousers around his ankles. All his efforts to look serious (walking briskly to meetings, handing reports to the boss with a flourish, working late on PowerPoint presentations) will be undone by the image of him breaking wind into a porcelain bowl.

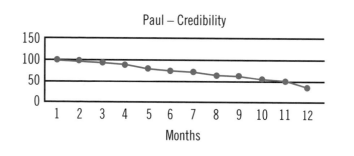

Paul – Credibility

The effectiveness of the method is in its repetition; it works best in the long term. Several months later, when your colleagues ask "Where is Paul" and you reply that he's in the toilet, they will end up thinking that he is not very effective because he spends half of his day sitting on the toilet rather than at his desk.

After a few months, some of your colleagues will begin to wonder why Paul's toilet trips take so long and conclude that he has a problem (painful constipation, difficulty pooing away from home, emotional blockage, explosive diarrhoea). You don't need to be a career management expert to see that Paul's prospects are diminishing while yours are ever increasing.

SCENARIOS

So that you completely understand this simple and very effective technique ("Where is Paul? / He's in the toilet") we will give you some scenario-based examples. For each of these examples Tom Hayatt will explain why the response is an effective way to discredit your colleague.

Question: Have you seen Paul?

Answer: Yes, five minutes ago, he was going to the toilet.

Tom Hayatt's analysis

I insist on the importance of repetition. This technique gives very good results in three to five months. A shorter period will probably not get the results you expect. You must let as many people in the company as possible think that Paul spends two to three hours a day in the bathroom.

Question: I have a call for Paul, does anyone know where he is?

Answer: He's been in the toilet for 30 minutes. Just tell the person that he's in a meeting and he'll call them back.

The trick is to give this response loud enough for the person on the other end of the phone to hear. The addition of "30 minutes" suggests that something abnormal is happening in the bathroom. If it is a client or one of the company's bosses calling, Paul will be discredited and that can only be good for you.

Question: We are in meeting room B3 and waiting for Paul to start the presentation, does anyone know where he is?

Answer: He told me he was going to the toilet and we should wait for him. I told him to join us in B3 when he's done.

Tom Hayatt's analysis

Here, you wait 20 to 30 minutes before going to inform Paul that his colleagues and manager are waiting for him in B3. All those present in the meeting room will picture Paul in the bathroom, and Paul's image is damaged yet again, but that is not the most ingenious part of this scenario. These people will then wait 20 to 30 minutes for Paul to arrive, wondering what he is doing in the toilet and after a while, they will think that he must have a problem (painful constipation, incontinence, no toilet paper). 20 to 30 minutes later, just after you have informed him that the boss is waiting for him to start the meeting, Paul will finally arrive. No one will ask him what happened in the bathroom. Who would ask: "Paul, are you constipated?" Paul will be looked at awkwardly at the time of his arrival but the meeting will start without anyone telling him anything. Your scheme will not be discovered. The credibility of Paul will have diminished in the eyes of ten people and that's what you wanted, right?

SCENARIO: The poisoned mug

Simple to implement, this powerful technique is for use when the employee you want to discredit is on leave. The best thing is that your target will never know he lost credibility during his vacation because of you.

World's best farter... oops father

SOLUTION: The generous gift

1. Confirm that the employee you want to discredit has gone on vacation.
2. The day after his departure, enter his office discreetly.
3. Prominently place a mug on his desk with a fart-related inscription. This mug will remain in place during his absence and people who visit his office will not fail to see this incriminating object. Choose an inscription suggesting that he received this mug as a gift from a family member or from one of his closest friends (people who know him well and know who he really is):

'I love my dad (even though he farts)'
'World's best farter... oops father'
'Fart downloading. Please wait...'
'I fart. What's your superpower?'

4. The day before the end of his holiday go back into his office and remove the mug.

Expert opinion

You can use a fart mug and get good results but be aware that there are many other objects that can discredit your colleague. Examples: a beautiful toilet brush still in its packaging, a pack of toilet deodorizers for 'strong odours' or one of these two excellent books – *How to Bonk at Work* or *How to Poo on Holiday*. Guaranteed Results. Remove these objects before he returns.

Testimonial

I successfully used this technique during my boss's holiday to try to take his place. I bought a big black notebook on which I wrote in large capital letters:

'MY POO AT WORK LOG'

I put the notebook in the middle of his office in full view. I filled about thirty pages of the journal, noting the date, time and any 'observations'. The entries were things like:

"Today I cannot go. Seven attempts and nothing but flatulence",
"Mexican Meal Tuesday = painful diarrhoea for three days",
"Inflammation and painful sitting position, I cancelled the meeting",
"3 farts released during the presentation",
"Abnormal colour and stench.
I must have a word with the wife tonight".

Pat, 31, paralegal, Slough

This strategy is very simple. You probably already know it and have used it among family or close friends. However, you've probably never dared to use it at work.

SOLUTION: Crowdpooping

1. You are talking to colleagues in a hallway, office or meeting room and need to release some gas.
2. Move your knee slightly to try not to make noise when you break wind.
3. VERY IMPORTANT: you must be the first to ask: "Has something died in here?"
4. Leave immediately, after stating that this is unacceptable and casting an accusing glare at the colleague who is competing with you for your next promotion.
5. It's as simple as that.

Expert opinion

I advise you to wait for the day when your farts smell really bad or search on the Internet for what kinds of food you should eat and combine to get smelly farts.

Testimonial

There were ten of us at the coffee machine talking business. I accused my colleague Martin. Everyone looked at him disapprovingly. The company boss was there. He asked Martin to go to the bathroom and to come back with some air freshener to disinfect the area he had polluted.

Stephen, 33, magazine editor, Croydon

SCENARIO: The letter of denunciation

To implement this technique, your company toilet must be equipped with stalls. You will have to observe the habits of the #1 or #2 of the employee you want to discredit beforehand. You need to know at what time he goes to the toilet each morning and what his favourite cubicle is. (When we go to do our deed at work, we are not adventurous, we all have a preferred cubicle where we go each day. He has one for sure.)

SOLUTION: Masquerade

1. Print out a company document where the name of the employee that you want to discredit appears clearly and in large letters. It can be a letter he received for example.
2. Once his #1 or #2 is in his cubicle, discreetly enter the bathroom and install yourself in the cubicle right next to him.
3. When you strip, put down several business items on the ground (laptop, file…) and put down the letter so that it protrudes under the partition. The #1 or the #2 who is in the cubicle next to you must be able to read the name on the document. Thus, he will think that it is your colleague who is in the cubicle next to him.

4. In order to tarnish the reputation of your colleague, you should behave in a way that breaks the golden rules. Try to release a couple of long, noisy farts, then a strained "nnnnmmmmmm" to indicate that you're having to push very hard. Motivate yourself, imitating your colleague's voice if you can: "Come on boy, let it go, you can do it, here she comes!".
5. Towards the end, lash out with your arms and legs to make the partition tremble and shout a victorious "woohoo!" to let everyone know you've just won the war against constipation.
6. Leave the toilets several minutes after the #1 or #2 has left the bathroom.

Expert opinion

After a few minutes, you can also say (in the voice of your colleague) "Wow, it's huge!", "Shit, there's no toilet paper, I'll have to use the bottom of my shirt again..."

Testimonial

I have used this technique 13 times in the last three months. The fourth month, my colleague was fired. The reason given by my company was "significant loss of productivity." For my part, I knew perfectly the reason for his departure.

Roland, 40, marketing assistant, Plymouth

While using the toilet, the seat comes apart.
Don't see this as a crisis, but an opportunity.

SOLUTION: The spider method

1. Leave the toilet with the broken toilet seat in your hand.
2. Ensure that Paul is away from his desk.
3. Find his desk, then throw the toilet seat on it with force.
4. Take a piece of paper and write in capital letters: "Paul, next time you break a toilet seat, get it fixed! Thank you."
5. Before leaving, say loudly: "I'm sure he's gone off to break another one, the imbecile!"

Expert opinion

This technique works with everything that you can break in a stall: the toilet paper dispenser, the toilet brush, the cistern, the door of the stall... Be imaginative!

Testimonial

I wanted to discredit my boss and a colleague. I couldn't decide who to blame so I to broke another toilet seat and left messages on two desks.

Simon, 42, car park manager, Abingdon

For this technique, you need to know at what time the employee you want to discredit goes to the toilet every day, and the cubicle he uses most often. You will also need a good screwdriver.

SOLUTION: DIY disaster

1. Just before he goes to the bathroom, go into the cubicle he always uses.
2. With your screwdriver, unscrew one of the elements in the cubicle so that the next user will encounter major difficulties.
3. We recommend partially unscrewing the toilet paper dispenser so it will fall loudly when he uses it.
4. You can also remove a small piece of the flush so that it does not work for the next user.
5. Unscrew the water supply so that the next time someone uses the flush, it creates a flood.
6. Unscrew the seat so that it detaches from the toilet when he sits on it.

Expert opinion

Why limit yourself to only one problem? I recommend giving your boss or colleague a couple of problems, if possible before an important meeting and at a time when he is in a hurry.

Testimonial

I am a good handyman. I had the idea to unscrew 90% of all the screws in the cubicle that my #3 uses. He is a total bastard. When he touched the toilet paper dispenser, the two walls and door fell apart, causing an incredible din. He ended up half naked, facing the company director who was in the bathroom at the same time (I'd predicted that, of course). I was there too but I had to get out of the bathroom quickly to laugh my ass off.

Kenneth, 32, Asia-Pacific accounts, Dover

To implement this technique, your company must have a front desk and employees working there.

SOLUTION: A load of poop

1. Place an order on behalf of a colleague and state that it needs to be dropped off at reception and the name of the final recipient must be inside the package. You want the contents to be brought to him at his desk by the receptionist so the other employees can see what his package contains.
2. Here is what it contains: 24 rolls of extra-soft toilet tissue for sensitive skin, 6 cans of industrial-strength air freshener, and 3 tubes of haemorrhoid cream.
3. Panicked on seeing these objects arrive at his desk, your colleague will certainly claim he never ordered these products. To ensure that the other employees are in no doubt that this package belongs to him, you should include one or two objects he frequently uses, his favourite Nespresso cartridges or whiteboard markers for example.

Expert opinion

Of course, you could simply place an order for 2,000 rolls of toilet paper. Just imagine Paul's face when he gets the call from reception: "Paul, a truck has just delivered 2,000 rolls of toilet paper for you. The boss is waiting in the lobby for you to explain the order. I've never seen him so angry."

Testimonial

The delivery arrived on his desk while our boss was in a meeting. The 70 employees in our open plan office bugged him for hours on end about why he'd ordered 48 rolls of toilet paper, 5 lavender deodorant sprays and 2 litres of haemorrhoid cream. When my boss got out of the meeting, things went from funny to hilarious. People were still chuckling at the disciplinary meeting.

George, assistant director, Stockton

SCENARIO: The invisible barrier

To implement this technique, you must know when your boss goes to the bathroom each day and his favourite cubicle. You will need three empty toilet rolls.

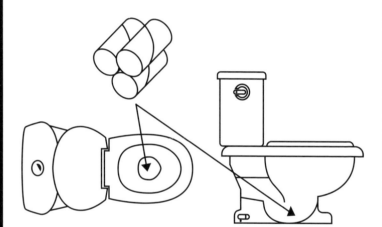

SOLUTION: Dambusters!

1. Five to ten minutes before your boss's trip to the bathroom, go to the stall he usually uses.
2. Place the three cardboard rolls at the bottom of the toilet bowl and push them into the U-bend with the brush so they clog up the pipe.
3. Leave the bathroom and go back to your desk. Your mission is complete.
4. Your boss will relieve himself and, when he flushes, he will clog the toilet. With any luck, the bowl will overflow. From your office, you can imagine him trying to push everything down the pipe with the brush.
5. After a few minutes, if the situation seems hopeless, it is possible that he will roll up his sleeves and try to solve the problem with his bare hands.
6. When he leaves, there is the possibility that someone will be waiting outside his stall. Your boss will have to explain that he has clogged the toilet. If the person waiting is his #1 or #2 or the director of the company, you can consider your mission accomplished.

Expert opinion

Instead of rolls, my wife uses five new tampons. They inflate quickly and work very well according to her. She has already stopped dozens of employees from progressing in the company with this technique.

Testimonial

The toilet overflowed. My boss returned with his beautiful £500 leather shoes ruined, a small piece of toilet paper stuck to the heel. The company director, who was passing by, asked him why he had wet feet. Panicking, he said he was very warm and when his feet overheated, they tended to sweat a lot!

Maggie, 43, billing services, Weston-Super-Mare

SCENARIO: The mayday SMS

This technique works particularly well in an open plan office. You are going to simulate that the employee you want to discredit is in distress and asking for help. In this example we shall, once again, call him 'Paul'.

Hello, I have a problem. I'm in the toilet. There is no toilet paper. Could you ask if anyone has a Kleenex? Thank you very much. It's very urgent.

Paul

SOLUTION: The phantom menace

1. Paul should not be in the vicinity when you apply this technique.
2. Take your smartphone in hand, stand up and address all employees who are in earshot: "I've just received a text message from Paul. It's a little embarrassing. He's in the bathroom and run out of toilet paper. He asks if anyone has a spare packet of Kleenex."
3. Your colleagues will be initially very surprised by your request. Seconds later, one of them will say that he has a Kleenex.
4. Say "I'll take it to him, I know where he is. He always goes to the bathroom on the top floor so he can't be heard."
5. Of course, you do not give Paul the tissues since he is not in the bathroom. He is actually in a meeting or the canteen or elsewhere in the company. But you are the only one who knows that.

Expert opinion

This is an excellent plan because, when the employee returns, no one will mention it. Nobody will say "I hear you were taking a dump and ran out of toilet paper, so you sent a mayday SMS asking for Kleenex." He will not know you've discredited him.

Note that there is a great variant: "I just received a text message from Paul, he's been locked in the bathroom for 3 hours and asks if anyone has a screwdriver?" This one is also very effective.

Testimonial

It was 3 p.m. My boss had left the office on an urgent family matter. He'd asked me to inform other members of his team that he was away. So I was the only one to know where he was. Just after he left, I applied the 'Mayday SMS' method. I said, "I received an SMS from the boss, he's in the toilet upstairs and having problems. The flush exploded when he pushed it. Yes, he wrote 'exploded'. He's clogged the toilet. He asks if anyone has a spare pair of trousers because they're completely soaked. He also wants a hairdryer." Of course no one had spare trousers to offer. As they did not see him for the rest of the afternoon my colleagues assumed he had gone home because of soiled pants and wet hair. In terms of loss of credibility, it was perfect.

David, 43, lawyer, Lincoln

SCENARIO: Spilled cup

To implement this technique, you need a cup filled with water. You will act just before an important meeting for the person you wish to discredit. For example, just before a presentation in front of the boss, or an appointment with an important client.

SOLUTION: Splash it all over

1. Go to see the employee you want to discredit with your cup of water in hand.
2. Discuss work for two or three minutes.
3. Stumble heavily on his waste-paper bin or a loose electric cable on the floor.
4. Spill your cup over his trousers, in the worst place. Pretend you are badly hurt so your colleagues believe it was an accident.
5. The water will give the impression that he has peed himself. He will be totally immobilized and unable to make his PowerPoint presentation or meeting with the boss.

Expert opinion

After such an occurrence, it is common for employees to dash to the bathroom, take off their trousers and attempt to dry them with the hand dryer. With luck, the employee will encounter his #1 or the boss taking a pee before the meeting.

Testimonial

I did not have a cup filled with water but did have coffee. It was very hot. My colleague is okay now, but received first degree burns in the worst possible place. He could not walk and was taken away 30 minutes later on a stretcher. Before the help arrived, we followed the advice of a doctor by phone. We had to pour a litre of cold water on the affected area every minute. I probably wouldn't try this again.

Simon, 42, car park manager, Abingdon

SCENARIO: Locked toilets

This is one of our favourite techniques, and a very efficient one. You need to know at precisely what time your target goes to the bathroom. You will also need a good screwdriver. Be patient and wait for the right time, even if it takes several months to set up.

SOLUTION: Lock, stock and block

1. Set up an important meeting with the #1, #2 and #3 of the person you wish to discredit (Paul). At this meeting, it is important that Paul has to give a presentation to the top management.
2. Set the time of the meeting 10 minutes after the time Paul usually goes to the bathroom.
3. 30 minutes before the meeting, go discreetly to the bathroom and, with your screwdriver, lock all the stalls from the outside.
4. Do the same to the doors in the bathroom on the floor above and the one below.
5. Paul will not be able to relieve himself before his presentation. Professional as ever, he will come to the meeting on time or a few minutes late – minutes he has spent trying every toilet door, praying that one of them finally opens.
6. He will make the presentation while squeezing his legs, grinning like an idiot, and discreetly trying to control his plumbing. For once, you will not be bored during a presentation.

Expert opinion

If you want someone to fail during a presentation, nothing is more efficient. If you really do not like Paul, wait an hour after the meeting before unlocking the doors of the toilets.

Testimonial

I locked half the cubicles and removed toilet paper from the others. I noticed that my colleague was not comfortable during his presentation but did not know if it was because he needed to go or because he felt sticky.

Frank, 34, major account manager, Chichester

SCENARIO: You leave traces of your trip behind

You finish your business, but have left the cubicle a total mess.
The toilet was clean before you entered.

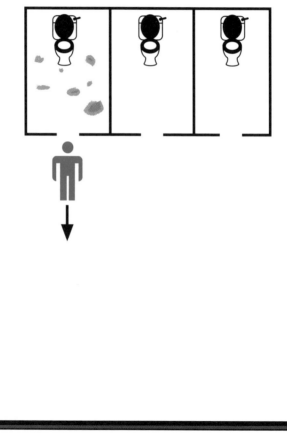

SOLUTION: Sign on the line

1. Take a felt-tip pen.
2. Above the sign that says 'Keep this place as clean as you found it', write: 'I found this place dirty, I left it dirty – did I do the right thing?'
3. Return to your desk immediately.
4. Send an email to the whole company. Subject: 'Toilet vandalism'.
5. In the email write: "One of you has left the toilet in an indefensible state and amused himself by writing a line of dubious humour on the sign. On behalf of the whole company, I would like to ask this person to start behaving like an adult in the toilet. P.S. Paul, we all know it was you. Admit it and I think many of us will respect you more."

Expert opinion

Being able to turn a crisis into an opportunity is a sign that you're destined for greatness.

Testimonial

Everybody was sure that the colleague I mentioned in the email was the one who did it. He's really had it in for me since then. I apologized to him and told him that while maybe I was wrong, I did this in good faith.

Chris, 28, book editor, London

To implement this technique, you'll need to be in a business where employees can place orders. You must also know the number that the employee you wish to discredit uses to place orders on the intranet.

SUPPLIES OR SPECIAL ORDERS REQUEST FORM
All special orders must have approval of Dept. Chair and Budget Officer

Department: Marketing   Date: 2016
Contact person: Paul   Telephone number: 00256 45 213
Approved by: Smith   Approved by: Smith
Received by: Paul

_____ Supplies Printing_____ Other _____

| Stock | Description of item | Qty | For office use only | | |
			Rec'd	B/O	Date B/O Rec'd
	Renova 3 ply toilet tissue roll	69			2016
	Poo pourri original toilet spray	1			2016
	WC odour blocker	1			2016
					Order filed by Paul

SOLUTION: The phantom paper purchaser

1. Fill out a request with the name of your colleague and his order number.
2. Each month, you will submit the same order with his name (Paul):
   1 x 3-ply rose pink macadamia skincare toilet tissue (60 Rolls - 5 packs of 12 Rolls each).
   1 x Poo Pourri toilet spray "Spritz the bowl before you go and no one else will ever know!"
   1 x Lavender & vanilla toilet odour blocker.
3. You will intercept the order on arrival so that Paul knows nothing.
4. In all companies, orders from employees are checked at regular intervals by the finance director. At some point your colleague or boss will be summoned to explain his order of luxury toilet rolls, anti-poo spray and toilet odour blocker.
5. Of course, at the meeting, he will deny having placed the order. But that is exactly what a guilty employee would do. Don't worry, he will be fired!

Expert opinion

Adding a tube of haemorrhoid cream to the order is an interesting idea. Employees who oversee orders will remember these details and draw conclusions: "Oh yeah, I remember he wanted to remain standing after his presentation" or "Now that I think about it, I've often seen him scratching his bum and during the last meeting he couldn't sit still."

Testimonial

I applied this method. It worked and my boss was fired but the media wanted to know why. I remember the article in *The Guardian:* "Despite his £5m salary, Mr. ***** was ordering luxury toilet tissue for home at the company's expense."

Andy, 42, financial analyst, Scarborough

SCENARIO: The thief of paper rolls and brush

This technique can be implemented in any type of company that uses lockers.

SOLUTION: Ali Baba's poop cavern

1. Each week steal several rolls of toilet paper and three brushes from the company bathroom.
2. The person you want to discredit (Paul) must have a locker for archiving his files that he rarely uses. You will need to open this locker during his absence and empty it discreetly.

3. Each week, fill the locker with the stolen toilet paper and brushes without Paul noticing.
4. Eventually someone in the company will realize that toilet paper and brushes are disappearing. An email will be sent out to let employees know that the theft of company property will result in bonuses being cut.
5. The day after this email, make an appointment with the company director and the top management in front of Paul's office. Tell them "I have found our thief."
6. Enter Paul's office, throw open the locker and expose the dozens of brushes and rolls of toilet paper. Say dramatically, "The thief of paper rolls and brushes is Paul!"
7. Of course Paul is going to deny everything, which is exactly what the thief would do. His career is over.

Expert opinion

During my first internship, I was not paid. To compensate, I stole everything I could from the company including toilet paper, actually huge industrial rolls, 80 cm in diameter. I was waiting for the evening to quietly leave the company with three large rolls before strapping them on the luggage rack of my moped.

Testimonial

I adopted a slightly different strategy to totally discredit my boss. We were not looking for a thief of loo rolls but for a thief of toilet seats. We found 14 in his locker and 28 in the boot of his company car.

Peter, 24, journalist, Belfast

Alone in a lift at work, you thought you were far from the noses and ears of your colleagues, so you broke wind. Bad luck, the elevator stops at an intermediate floor and your boss walks into the elevator. Do not panic, this is actually a great opportunity to discredit a colleague.

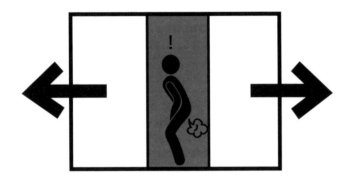

SOLUTION: Sleight of wind

1. Do not push your boss away, shouting: "Don't come in here! I farted three times and the smell is unbearable!"
2. Instead say: "Good to see you, may I ask your opinion? There's a strange smell in here and I cannot tell what it is."
3. Your boss will sniff and say: "Obviously, it's the stench of flatulence."
4. Answer: "That's exactly what I thought. Paul left the elevator as I got in. He looked rather anxious and I couldn't figure out why."
5. Shut up. Do not add anything. The damage is done.

Expert opinion

This is physics that everyone will understand: a fart will be felt more intensely in a lift. The reason is the limited space and lack of ventilation. According to an American study, if 12 people fart in a lift, it will catch fire if one of them were to light a cigarette; hence the ban on smoking in elevators since 1934, when the first incident of this type occurred.

Testimonial

My boss is a keen hunter. I asked him about the strange smell, he said it smelled of boar.

Daniel, 36, legal expert, Penzance

SCENARIO: The small toilet poster

To implement this technique, you need a company bathroom, a printer and some sticky tape. You are going to create a small poster for the toilet and sign it with the name of your boss or the person you wish to discredit.

SOLUTION: Sign me up

1. Open Word. Choose a serious font.
2. Create one of notices below, print it and sign it with the name of the person you wish to discredit.

   "Toilet paper is very expensive and we are trying to save the company money. With immediate effect we are limiting the supply to one sheet per employee per visit. Paul."

   "PRIVATE BATHROOM. To keep this bathroom clean, it is now reserved for senior management only. If you're not member of senior management, please use the public toilets which are located on the High Street, just 500m from this building. Paul."

3. The first sign makes Paul look a fool, while the second one is sure to ignite a class war in your company. In both cases, Paul will deny being the author of the posters. But that's exactly what you'd expect from a sneaky, elitist troublemaker like him.

Expert opinion

I collect toilet posters. When I see one, I take it and put it in an album. I have 258 of them. The oldest was created on a typewriter in 1933 and I bought it for $789 on eBay.

Testimonial

I used both posters signed by my boss, two weeks apart. Before taping up the second poster, I installed a chrome brush, luxury toilet seats and expensive toilet paper. Senior management were delighted, until the rest of the workforce went on strike.

Michael, 22, courier, Luton

SCENARIO: The office smells bad

To implement this method, you need the person you wish to discredit to be out of the office.

VENI

VIDI

VICI

SOLUTION: The time bomb

1. As soon as the person you want to discredit goes away, sneak quietly into his office without being seen. Once there, release one or two farts. Do this as often as possible.
2. You must ensure that his office windows are closed and that the air conditioning is on the minimum setting.
3. The gas will accumulate in the office and when a colleague or your boss goes in during his absence, they'll find that the room stinks.
4. Your target will soon be known in the company as the employee whose office smells. It is not a great way to get promoted.

Expert opinion

If you do well, in just three or four days, the air in the office will become unbreathable. It usually takes only two weeks for the nickname of the employee to become 'Stinky Fartman'.

Testimonial

I used this method in the office of a colleague. The day he came back, my boss took him to see a doctor to discuss his problem. He also decided that he would no longer go out to meet clients. He is still dealing, but only by phone.

Henry, 43, estate agent, Wrexham

SCENARIO: The flush does not work

After the deed is done, you realize that the flush doesn't work. This not a problem, this is a great opportunity! You will now know and understand why.

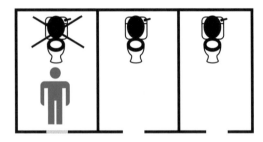

SOLUTION: The Post-it of remorse

1. First, try three or four more times. You never know.
2. Take a sticky note from your bag and write: "I am so sorry; I didn't know the flush was broken. I feel terrible." Sign it with a colleague's name (Paul).
3. Stick the sticky note on the wall as visible as possible. Close the toilet lid.
4. Leave the toilet, head held high, as if you only just arrived. If someone comes in, say: "No, use the other one! Paul broke that one."
5. Go to Paul's desk and reprimand him loudly: "This is the third time you've broken the toilet flush! You have to stop." Then add: "How old are you?"

Expert opinion

Are there still people out there who do not check in advance that the flush operates? This is something so basic that we should not need to remind you of it any more. And if you get the bright idea to take up plumbing and fix the flush, I do not know where to begin listing the problems that could lead to. Would you really like to risk drenching yourself at work? Don't do silly things when you have the opportunity to discredit a colleague!

Testimonial

I used to be completely distraught before I learned this one: I quietly closed the lid to hide my deed and tiptoed out in the hope that nobody would see. But there is always someone waiting to use your cubicle, so I always had to explain in embarrassment that I clogged up the toilet. Since I learned this method, I've never fallen into that trap and I don't have to change companies every six months.

Ben, 37, manager, Brisbane

SCENARIO: The toilet brush manual

To implement this method, you must be in a large company looking to save money. You can use this method to discredit a colleague, your manager or even the director of your company.

NOTICE

Read and understand operator's manual and all other safety instructions before using this equipment

SOLUTION: Manual assistance

1. In PowerPoint, create a manual 'How to use a toilet brush like a pro'. 10 pages – containing diagrams, instructions and tips for a more efficient use of the toilet brush.
2. Sign it with the name of the colleague you want to discredit (Paul).
3. In the introduction to this manual, write: "As you know, to improve our competitiveness, our company is trying to make savings. We are a company of 1,580 employees and I calculate that if we all used the toilet brushes more often and more effectively, we could fire two cleaning ladies. I think I know a thing or two about toilet brushes and I spent a week creating this manual to share my best tips with you. I hope you will read it carefully and you will apply the methods that I have invented. Together we can make a difference with our toilet brush. Paul."
4. The next day, come into work at 5:30 a.m. and print 1,580 copies of Paul's manual. Deliver the copies to the desk of every employee before they arrive. It will be difficult for Paul to convince 1,580 people that he is not the author.

Expert opinion

If you write such a manual, send it to me. I invented some effective techniques such as the hot toilet brush (incorporating a hand dryer) and the Niagara Falls (or 360° toilet brush) but I'm always interested in tips from other users.

Testimonial

This totally backfired. The boss thought the manual was brilliant and congratulated the manager I wanted to discredit. He asked him to make two other manuals. The manager did not dare tell him that he was not the author.

Paul, 57, account manager, Inverness

SCENARIO: You create odours

You have just finished, and you leave an unpleasant odour behind.
You leave the toilet and run into the boss of the company, who is clearly
on his way to the same cubicle. Most employees panic in this situation
but this is actually an opportunity.

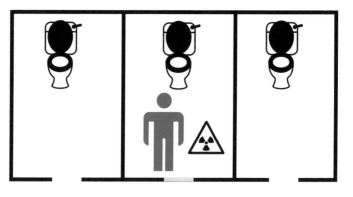

SOLUTION: The blame game

1. Keep walking towards the boss.
2. With an expression of horror, tell him that someone has left a dreadful smell in the toilet.
3. If possible, blame the person you wish to discredit and who could be a plausible culprit. Say, for example: "I think it was Paul, he ran out when I came in."
4. If the smell is unbearable, make sure you acknowledge that you too could not go in because of it.

Expert opinion

I advise you to spray air freshener on Paul's coat when he is not around. This is an NLP technique. Other employees will associate Paul with the bathroom without being able to explain why.

Testimonial

I know that my boss goes to poo at 11.00 a.m. every day. So, I've trained myself to go at 10.50 and leave a horrible odour behind every time. I enjoy waiting for my boss to enter the bathroom just so I can tell him: "Martin, again!"

Liam, 38, consultant, Canterbury

SCENARIO: When all else fails

So, you have adopted our strategies, but they have not worked out. Another employee was promoted in your place. You have one last chance: a campaign of harassment so he resigns and you can take his position.

So, how will the clever new boss who says he has a solution for every problem deal with this one?

SOLUTION: Roll with it

1. You need to know when the employee goes to the bathroom and which cubicle he uses.
2. Just before he arrives, empty the toilet paper rolls.
3. On the cardboard rolls, write a message he will discover once he has finished: "So, how will the clever new boss who says he has a solution for every problem deal with this one?"
4. Do it every day with new sentences "What would the God of marketing do in this situation?"

Expert opinion

You could try horror movie-themed variations like: "I know what you did last Summer... and yesterday in the bathroom".

Testimonial

I applied this method for a month. The employee was on edge and went crying to the boss with nine empty toilet rolls. But the boss did not take him seriously, he even laughed out loud at the last inscription I had left, "What would MacGyver do?"

Jeff, 37, geological surveyor, Redbridge

HOW TO USE THE URINALS AGAINST A COLLEAGUE

The urinals are also governed by unbreakable rules. You can never look into the eyes of the person standing next to you. Similarly, you must not start a conversation with another user (in any case, he will not respond). You must not express your feelings (such as sighing in relief). Stay calm and composed whatever may happen. Do not excuse yourself if you commit an error (flatulence, bad aim). Always maximize the difference with other users.

Example 1

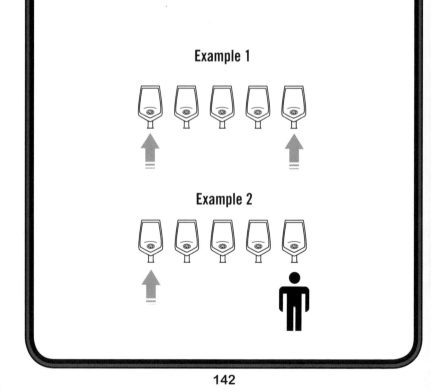

Example 2

SOLUTION: Peeing in the Wind

Here is how you can discredit a colleague with the urinals.

1. Tell him: "I just met the big boss in the bathroom."
2. "He was at the urinals, so I was a bit nervous."
3. "But I chose the urinal right next to his and just started talking."
4. "We were shoulder to shoulder, keeping firm eye-contact the whole time while we peed."
5. "He said he appreciated my directness and I even got my 10% salary increase just by asking!"
6. Of course, all of this is complete fabrication but you can be sure that your colleague will try to re-enact what you have told him to get a salary increase.
7. The boss will find this behaviour very awkward. Paul will never get promoted.

Example 3

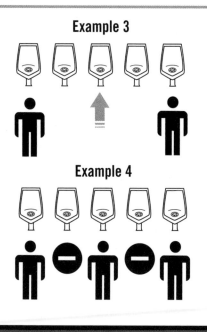

Example 4

CONCLUSION

Thanks to the sharp observations and erudite advice of Tom Hayatt, your poos at work will never again hinder your career development. Now that you have all the knowledge, you are among the best pooers in the UK. If you dreaded it before, we now hope you will enjoy pooing at work. And always keep in mind that you are getting paid while you do it!

Here is how your monthly salary should increase in the coming years.

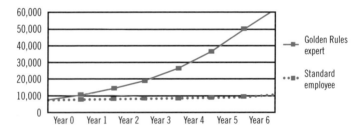

However, based on our thorough observations of the behaviour of people who buy self-improvement books, almost 99% have the disturbing tendency to endlessly accumulate books that are supposed to help them with their career, without ever putting their advice into practice. Endlessly gathering theoretical knowledge on a subject without moving on to practice is exactly the same as trying to learn how to drive a car by reading books about cars and driving techniques. It is completely useless.

This book gives you the best information to poo your way to the top – this is not the kind of self-help book that gives advice on how to dramatically change your life that is impossible to implement. Our techniques are easy. Our readers are the ones with the fastest salary increases in United Kingdom. Our guide has been conceived in a way that allows you to start applying its advice today – and get real benefits from it. Using our techniques will significantly increase your salary in coming years!